Adverbs Say

"FINALLY!"

by Michael Dahl   illustrated by Maira Chiodi

PICTURE WINDOW BOOKS
a capstone imprint

Right. You were probably expecting adverbs.

Adverbs *are* in the title of this book.

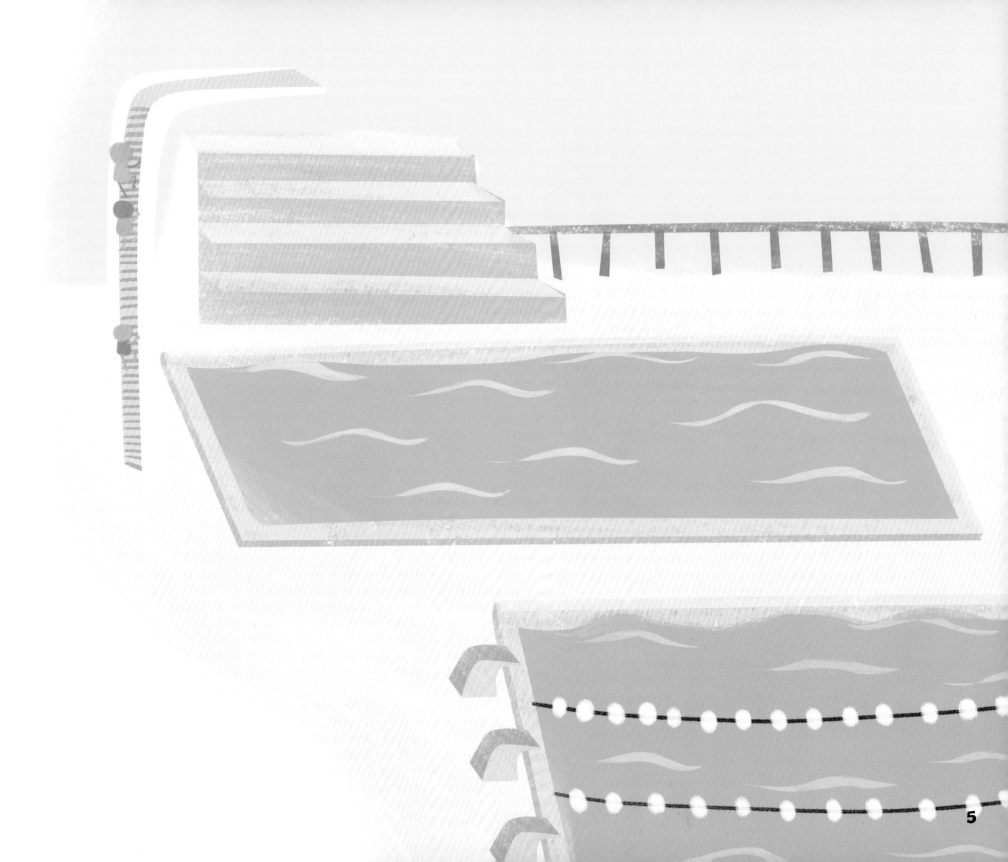

Verbs are parts of speech that usually tell us something happened. Adverbs tell us *how* something happened.

6

"See" and "climb" are the verbs. Adverbs tell us *how* we see and *how* we climb—clearly, quickly, and so slowly!

Adverbs can describe how we do things.

Climb **swiftly**!

I'm climbing as **rapidly** as I can!

I'm climbing up **cautiously**. And I'm looking down **nervously**.

9

Adverbs can describe how we say something.

Adverbs can describe physical actions. They tell us how we move.

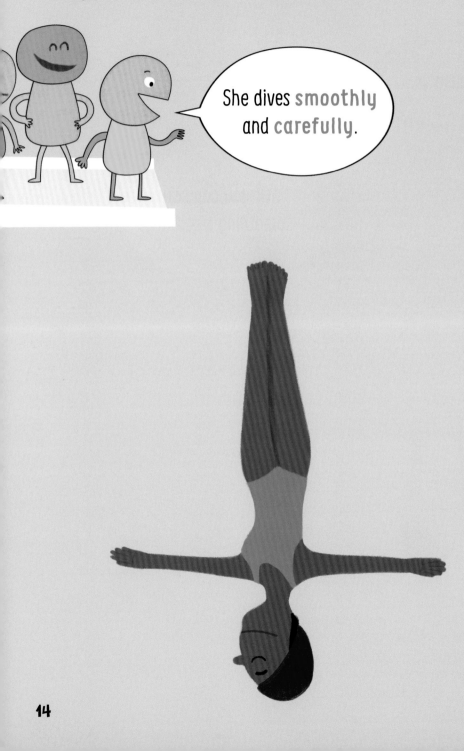

She dives smoothly and carefully.

And he dives beautifully.

Ooh! She dives **fiercely**!

He dives **poorly** but **stylishly**!

Some adverbs tell us how often something is done.

Most adverbs aren't content to lie around.
They like to be where the action is.

Adverbs can be at the front, middle, or end of a sentence.

You can spot many adverbs by their ending.

21

Some adverbs tell us when something takes place.

Adverbs can also help adjectives describe things better.

Adverbs make sentences more interesting.

And so the adverb sat there **silently** . . . **thoroughly** wet . . . and **miserably** cold.

ALL ABOUT AMAZING ADVERBS

⭐ Adverbs are words that describe or modify verbs, adjectives, or even other adverbs.

I ran QUICKLY through the dark forest. (modifies the verb "ran"; *How did I run?*)
I dropped my VERY shiny penny into the wishing well. (modifies the adjective "shiny"; *How shiny?*)
The giant yelled SO LOUDLY! (the adverb "so" modifies the adverb "loudly"; *How loudly?*)

⭐ Adverbs can tell us *how* something is done.

The baby giraffe walked AWKWARDLY.
The tree fell NOISILY to the ground.

⭐ Adverbs can tell us *when* something happens.

I rode the school bus YESTERDAY.
She will climb the volcano TOMORROW.
They woke up EARLY to catch some worms.

⭐ Some adverbs tell us *how often* something happens.

He NEVER shares his chocolate treats with me.
SOMETIMES it snows in April.

⭐ Many adverbs end in the letters "ly."

⭐ The following words are adverbs that commonly modify other adverbs:
"almost," "always," "definitely," "really," "so," "too," and "very."

ABOUT THE AUTHOR

Michael Dahl is the author of more than 200 books for children and has won the AEP Distinguished Achievement Award three times for his nonfiction. He is the author of the bestselling *Bedtime for Batman* and *You're a Star, Wonder Woman!* picture books. He has written dozens of books of jokes, riddles, and puns. He likes to play with words. In grade school, he read the dictionary for fun. Really. Michael is proud to say that he has always been a noun. A PROPER noun, at that.

ABOUT THE ILLUSTRATOR

Maira Chiodi's colorful, joyful work has appeared in magazines, books, games, and a variety of other products. As a child in Brazil, Maira spent hours cutting paper, painting, and reading—creating wildly imaginative worlds all her own. Today she feels lucky to be able to create and share her illustrations and designs with kids and grown-ups around the world. She divides her time between Canada and Brazil, finding inspiration for her art in nature, animation, and the culture of her native country.

GLOSSARY

action—the act of doing something

adjective—a word that tells more about a noun or pronoun

adverb—a word that describes or modifies a verb, an adjective, or another adverb

describe—to tell about something

modify—to change or provide further detail about something

physical—having to do with something that can be seen and touched

verb—a word that shows an action or state of being (how something is, was, or will be)

THINK ABOUT IT

1. What adverbs could you use to describe how a songbird sings? (Hint: Think about words ending in "ly.")

2. What adverbs could you use to describe how a racehorse runs?

3. What adverbs could you use to modify the adjectives in this sentence? The _____ small mouse fought the _____ big lion. Give at least three examples for each blank.

READ MORE

Heinrichs, Ann. *Adverbs.* Language Rules. New York: AV2 by Weigl, 2018.

Loewen, Nancy. *The Big Problem (and the Squirrel Who Eventually Solved It): Understanding Adjectives and Adverbs.* Language on the Loose. North Mankato, MN: Picture Window Books, a Capstone imprint, 2016.

Riggs, Kate. *Adverbs.* Grammar Basics. Mankato, MN: Creative Education, 2013.

INTERNET SITES

Enchanted Learning: Grammar: Adverb
https://www.enchantedlearning.com/grammar/partsofspeech/adverbs/index.shtml

Grammaropolis: The Adverbs
https://www.grammaropolis.com/adverb.php

Schoolhouse Rock: Adverbs
https://www.youtube.com/watch?v=dDwXHTcodNg

LOOK FOR ALL THE PARTS OF SPEECH TITLES

INDEX

Editor: Jill Kalz
Designer: Lori Bye
Production Specialist: Katy LaVigne
The illustrations in this book were created digitally.

Picture Window Books are published by Capstone
1710 Roe Crest Drive, North Mankato, Minnesota 56003
www.capstonepub.com

Library of Congress Cataloging-in-Publication Data is available on the Library of Congress website.
ISBN 978-1-5158-3872-2 (library binding)
ISBN 978-1-5158-4061-9 (paperback)
ISBN 978-1-5158-3877-7 (eBook PDF)
Summary: Whether diving from a very tall platform or crossing the finish line after a really grueling bike race, the adverbs have the perfect word: *finally*! Honestly, isn't it time for a quirky parts-of-speech adventure that subtly teaches grammar basics while readers are busy cheering loudly and giggling often?

All internet sites appearing in back matter were available and accurate when this book was sent to press.

Printed and bound in China.
001654